FIGHTER
AIRCRAFT

Bill Gunston

TREASURE
PRESS

CONTENTS

The Sopwith Pup of 1916 (left) was one of the sweetest of all fighters to fly. This is a modern replica. The fighter on the previous page is a Vought F-8 Crusader, used by the US Navy. The endpapers illustrate the most versatile modern warplane, the Panavia Tornado IDS.

INTRODUCTION

Aircraft, in the form of balloons, were first used in war for observational purposes in 1793. Aeroplanes joined the fray in North Africa in the autumn of 1911. This conflict between the Italians, who had aeroplanes, and the Turks, who did not, resulted in much pioneer development of aerial reconnaissance and bombing, but no air combat was possible. A few visionaries suggested that hostile flying machines would eventually try to interfere with aerial reconnaissance and bombing, but at the outbreak of World War I in August 1914 the official view totally discounted and ignored such a possibility. Indeed, the Royal Flying Corps pilots and observers, who stretched air navigation to its limits by flying to France in the first week of that war, had caused some embarrassment by asking 'What do we

do if we meet a Zeppelin?' Some of them were given rifles and ammunition, but the official view was that a brave crew might try crashing into the airship as a means of bringing it down.

As early as 1912 aircraft designers had considered aeroplanes intended for combat. Vickers had produced an EFB (Experimental Fighting Biplane), which was exhibited at Olympia in London in 1913, and at the same time the Royal Aircraft Factory had flown the first FE.2 (Farman Experimental, which simply meant it had a pusher propeller behind the wings). Both aircraft adopted the pusher configuration chiefly so that a gun could be fired from the nose, though a search of the patent literature would have revealed several suggestions for controlling a machine-gun so that it could fire its bullets between the blades of a revolving propeller. One of the inventors of such an interrupter or synchronizing gear was the French designer Raymond Saulnier. His chief test-pilot, Roland Garros, despaired of official interest in such a device and in April 1915 went into battle with steel deflectors fixed to his tractor propeller. Quickly he ran up a succession of victories. Then, by extraordinary ill-luck, his aircraft fell into German hands. The Dutch designer, Anthony Fokker, who had a factory in Germany,

The latest in a series of very successful fighters from the French Dassault company, the Mirage 2000 (below), is here surrounded by some of the weapons it can carry.

was asked to copy Garros' scheme, but instead he made and tested an interrupter gear which he fitted to one of his E-series (Eindecker = monoplane) scouts. Leutnant Oswald Boelcke was selected to try it out, and he soon became the first ace (a pilot with five confirmed victories). Subsequently Boelcke went from strength to strength, writing a code of practice for aerial fighting and hand-picking pilots to form a crack fighter unit. When he was killed in October 1916 he had shot down 40 Allied aircraft.

By 1917 the fighter had become fairly standard as a neat single-seat biplane with a tractor propeller and two synchronized machine-guns. Fighter squadrons changed little in the following 20 years, apart from a steady increase in engine power, but by the late 1930s two influences were evident. All-metal stressed-skin construction favoured the change to the aerodynamically clean cantilever monoplane with about 1000 horsepower, enclosed cockpit and retractable landing gear; and most

nations introduced long-range twin-engined fighters, usually with a crew of two, primarily to escort bombers. The first year of World War II was to demonstrate that the twin-engined fighters, such as the Messerschmitt Bf 110, were in general unable to survive in dogfights, but the invention of radar and the desperate need in 1940 to intercept bombers at night led to a new fighter – the radar-equipped interceptor. Whereas most fighters remained single-seat, single-engined machines, which 'tangled' with their opponents in close combat, the night interceptor used the newly developed airborne radar to find its prey by night. Most night-fighter victims never knew what hit them.

By the end of World War II the machine-gun had been replaced by powerful cannon, and in fighters the propeller was being replaced by the turbojet. In the United States further electronic wizardry by 1949 resulted in airborne systems – at that time large, heavy and temperamental – with which an interceptor could find a target at night or in bad

weather, and shoot it down without the fighter pilot ever seeing it. At first guns were used, then spin-stabilized rockets and, by 1955, guided missiles. By the mid-1950s galloping technology had led to dramatic advances in propulsion, structures, aerodynamics and the emerging science of avionics (aviation electronics), which had taken the speed of fighters past Mach 1 (the speed of sound) and on to Mach 2. It had also resulted in a proliferation of guided missiles for many purposes, so that the British government erroneously stated in April 1957 that the RAF would be 'unlikely to require' any more fighters. Missiles would be bought instead.

This policy was eventually seen to be nonsense, but the fighter did undergo a further change. In the 1950s ground attack missions had been flown by fighters originally designed for air combat, but today most small warplanes are designed specially for attack on surface targets. Some have little or no air-to-air capability, and so can hardly be called fighters. A few purpose-built air-combat aircraft exist, characterized by powerful engines and large wings in relation to their overall size and weight. Countries with large airspace (such as Britain, which has to defend airspace from Iceland to the Baltic Sea) need long-endurance and comprehensively equipped interceptors which, with powerful radar and missiles, can destroy hostile aircraft up to 150km (96 miles) away from the fighter.

A British fighter of World War II was the Spitfire IA (left) seen here with a turret-armed Defiant and a Tempest. Japan's A6M 'Zero' is pictured (above).

WORLD WAR I

In 1914 nobody knew how a fighter should be arranged. Inventors had devised ways of allowing a machine-gun to fire safely past the blades of a revolving propeller, but most of the early war aircraft were pushers, with the propellers at the back. In June 1915, however, the German Fokker monoplanes (below) began to score.

Before 1914 the fastest aircraft were French monoplanes, among them the products of the Morane-Saulnier company. From these was developed the excellent Type N, or MS.5 (*top left*) of 1914, which with an engine of 110hp could reach 165km/h (103mph). The Moranes were tested and demonstrated by Garros who, after he got into uniform with the Aviation Militaire, fixed a machine-gun to fire straight ahead (in a different type of Morane) and then was shot down over Germany and so gave the game away. From that time on, air combat was a deadly game.

Some of the old pushers, with either a fixed forward-firing gun or a gunner aiming a weapon from a nose cockpit, continued to play a major role. Among them was the Airco D.H.2 (*above*), which was a single-seater. At first its pilots had to fly the aircraft and aim the machine-gun, as well as from time to time change the heavy drums of ammunition. The obvious answer was to fix the gun to fire ahead and aim the whole aircraft, and by the end of 1915 this had become the universal method of aerial fighting. Even today, aiming the aircraft in order to fire a gun is the common close-range method.

Typical of the later breed of World War I fighters was the French Spad VII (*left*). The development of more powerful engines, in this case a 150hp V-8 Renault (later improved to deliver 235hp), allowed fighters to be much heavier and tougher and to carry more than one machine-gun. Some of the 14,400 Spads had a heavy-calibre cannon which fired shells through the centre of the propeller. A single good hit could bring down an opponent, but the gun's size, weight, recoil and choking fumes were real drawbacks.

Today we are so used to monoplanes that we may think designers in the early days were foolish to use a greater number of wings. But today's streamlined aircraft were then impossible. A monoplane had to be festooned with projecting posts and bracing wires, and careful testing seemed to show that the biplane, made like a strong box tightened up with diagonal bracing wires, was a better all-round type of aeroplane than the monoplane. Another factor was that, as it had to have the same total wing area, the monoplane tended to have a greater span. This usually made it less agile than the more compact biplane. Designer Herbert Smith at the Sopwith company took this thinking still further and wondered if with three-wings a fighter could do even better. In May 1916 he completed the first Sopwith Triplane, and when it reached the Royal Naval Air Service squadrons on the Western Front in November 1916, it threw the enemy into such a panic that

within a few weeks 14 German and Austrian companies were building triplane fighters. By far the most famous was the Fokker Dr.I (*right*), a crimson example of which was flown by Baron Manfred von Richthofen, Germany's greatest ace and today popularly known as 'The Red Baron'.

On 21 April 1918 this scourge of Allied flyers, with 80 confirmed victories, fell, shot through the head by a single bullet from Roy Brown of 209 Squadron RAF (the RAF had been formed three weeks previously). No. 209 Squadron flew the greatest of all World War I fighters, the biplane Sopwith Camel (*below*). For nearly 60 years it was officially stated that the Camel had a record score of 1,294 confirmed victories. A British author, Chaz Bowyer, proved that the Camels of the British squadrons alone had a total score exceeding 2,800. Even this total was surpassed by several types in World War II.

At the start of World War I the most numerous category of aero engine was the rotary type, in which the cylinders are arranged radially like the spokes of a wheel (like modern radial engines) but rotated around a fixed crankshaft. The propeller was fastened to the spinning engine. The idea was that making the engine rotate would improve cooling and make heavy and vulnerable water-cooling unnecessary. But as the war progressed, the in-line and V-type water-cooled engines – more nearly resembling car engines – improved dramatically, while the rotaries suffered from basic limitations. Thus, while the two famous scouts on the previous pages were powered by rotary engines, the later machines shown here had fixed water-cooled engines.

Water-cooled engines eventually looked streamlined, but in these early installations a large cooling radiator was placed square-on, immediately behind the propeller. Other 1917 aircraft had radiators on the sides, underneath, or even recessed into the top wing. In the latter position, if bullets punctured the radiator, the pilot could be covered with scalding water.

Perhaps the best of all the British fighting scouts serving in numbers on the Western Front was the S.E.5a (*top left*). This was one of the many types designed at the Royal Aircraft Factory at Farnborough by Capt. Geoffrey de Havilland and Harry Folland. Its engine was the French Hispano-Suiza V-8 of 150hp, but this was soon replaced by the 200hp version with a reduction gear to drive a larger propeller more slowly. The reduction gear was unreliable and after serious delays a British development of the engine, the Wolseley Viper, was substituted. The S.E. thereafter did splendidly, an especially popular quality being its structural strength. It could even be dived vertically down at full throttle. Something like 5,000 were built.

Fastest of all the World War I scouts was the Italian Ansaldo SVA series (*bottom left*). These were designed as single-seat fighters, and were generally capable of the remarkable speed of 230km/h (143mph), but in service they were often used for reconnaissance, bombing and even training. The aircraft shown is, in fact, a two-seat trainer, designated SVA.9, powered by a 250hp Isotta-Fraschini V-6 engine. Unlike most of the World War I aircraft illustrated in this book it is a true original, carefully restored in Italy in the 1960s. Restoring old fighters, or building convincing replicas, was unknown until the 1960s. In Texas there is a whole air force of restored combat aircraft, and smaller versions of famous fighters are now being made that people can afford to fly.

BETWEEN THE WARS

Between the two world wars fighters were subjected to a vast amount of experimentation. Like this Bristol Bulldog of the RAF, which was in front-line service from 1929 until 1937, most fighters continued to be fabric-covered biplanes armed with two rifle-calibre machine-guns. Then from 1937 the scene was transformed by the smooth monoplane with more power and vastly heavier armament.

A few manufacturers persisted with monoplane fighters even in the 1920s. One of them was the Frenchman Emile Dewoitine (pronounced De-wut-een), who had been a fighter designer in World War I. He formed his own company in 1920. The French Navy bought 29 of his first post-war monoplane fighters, and of the many versions, hundreds were sold to other countries, especially to Switzerland, and considerable numbers were constructed under licence in Italy and Argentina. His own government, however, showed so little interest that in 1928 he shut his factory in Toulouse and moved to Switzerland. There he created a fine series of fighters, all of them made of metal and with a parasol wing – a monoplane wing carried on struts above the fuselage. The best known of the Swiss designs was the D 27 (below). The engine was a 600hp Hispano-Suiza V-12, and an unusual feature was that the fuel was carried in a tank which formed the underside of the centre fuselage. In emergency this tank could be jettisoned, an idea which became common in World War II.

The Swiss federal workshops at Thun built 85, of which 66 were used from 1930 onwards by the Swiss air force; one of these is pictured (right) at a flying display in the 1970s. The maximum speed was about 315km/h (196mph), an excellent figure for the time. Another modern feature was the skinning of light alloy, which made these monoplanes tough and well able to remain serviceable over long periods of arduous use.

Both aircraft shown here are almost exactly as they were built. The D 26 (right) is a much less powerful machine with an American Wright radial engine of 250hp. Most of the D 26s were used as advanced trainers, but after World War II a number survived doing duty as tugs for sailplanes. No. 282 is still flying, and was photographed recently looking almost as if it was still a fighter in the front line of air combat.

Today Boeing is by far the largest and best-known constructor of civil transport aircraft, but 50 years ago the company was famed for its pursuits – the former American name for fighters. The first version of an extremely important series was the P-12 (*below right*), a traditional biplane but with a welded steel tube fuselage and one of the new Pratt & Whitney Wasp engines. This 1929 fighter, seen in the markings of the 95th Pursuit Squadron, US Army, led to many other versions of the P-12, and then in 1933 to the P-26 (*below*), a racy little monoplane with a stressed-skin structure but still with a Wasp engine. This beautifully restored example is wearing the Thunderbird insignia of the US Army's 34th Squadron.

One of the last biplane fighters was the British Gloster Gladiator (*right*). Designed to a 1930 specification, it did not reach the RAF until late 1937, by which time it was becoming obsolete. Powered by the excellent 840hp Bristol Mercury engine (fine for 1930 but nothing like enough for 1940), it was armed with four machine-guns and had a sliding hood over the cockpit. Gladiators, and the naval Sea Gladiator, fought in the Norwegian campaign and in the defence of Malta in 1940. The only flying Gladiator in the world, this one is painted in the red/blue stripe of 72 Squadron.

ARMAMENT

Clearly the question of armament is central to any fighter aircraft. In the early days the machine-gun was dominant and its larger descendants are important to this day, though missiles are also usually carried. Electronic devices, though they do not 'shoot', are also included here because without them no modern fighter could survive, let alone conquer airspace.

GUNS

By 1912 enterprising young military pilots had fired their revolvers, pistols or rifles in the air, usually at ground targets. But it was soon recognized that, as in the trenches, the dominant weapon was the machine-gun. For aerial use it had to be air-cooled and as light as possible. The pivoted weapons, which were aimed by the observer, had separate replaceable magazines, important types being the British Lewis (actually an American gun made in Belgium), the French Hotchkiss and the German Parabellum. When a gun was fixed to fire ahead, it could be fed with a long belt; the most important Allied fixed gun was the Vickers, and for the Germans the Spandau. All fired at a cyclic rate of about 550 shots per minute, but it was not common for any gun to be on target for more than a second or two at a time.

From 1912 a minor proportion of the guns used in aircraft were of a heavier calibre. Most of these shell-firing 'cannon' were made by Hotchkiss with various barrel lengths and calibres (37mm was most common) and fed by a clip of ammunition. Germany also developed several cannon; the only one in wide use was the 20mm Becker installed on pivoted mountings. It protected heavy bombers. The most popular Vickers was generally of 7.7mm (0.303in) calibre, but a few were scaled up to larger sizes. Likewise, the excellent belt-fed gun developed by Browning in the United States (normally of 7.62mm (0.3in)

calibre) appeared by the end of the war, in 12.7mm (0.5in) calibre, but only slowly gained acceptance. Large calibre recoilless guns, which fired a counterweight or gas jet to the rear, were important in Britain and the Soviet Union but were abandoned by 1935.

During the 1920s a wealth of automatic weapons was accepted by various air forces. FN in Belgium, which made the Lewis and Browning, developed its own improved versions, while Madsen in Denmark produced important guns, especially cannon of 23mm and other calibres. In Switzerland Oerlikon (Bührle & Co. perfected a series of rather low-powered cannon, mainly of 20mm calibre, derived from the German Semag, itself based on the Becker. Germany adopted the Oerlikon and from 1935 it was made in quantity by Ikaria and other companies. The Hispano-Suiza company developed its more powerful 20mm gun and had it accepted by many nations including, by 1939, Britain, which set up British MARC Ltd to make it under licence. Britain also adopted the American Browning, though modified to fire 0.303in ammunition. But Germany led the way in World War II with a series of dramatic new guns, most important of which was the Mauser MG 213 with a revolver-type feed cylinder. After the war this was the starting point for the American 20mm MG 39, the French DEFA and the British Aden (both of 30mm) and the Mauser also influenced the excellent Russian guns.

In 1952 US General Electric literally revolutionized aircraft guns with the multi-barrel cannon resembling the Gatling of a century earlier. Designated M61 or T-171, it fired at rates up to 6000 per minute. Subsequent versions were driven electrically, hydraulically or self-powered by the ammunition. Some came in rifle calibre and others up to 30mm, such as the GAU/8 tank-killer, most powerful of all aircraft guns.

STALLATIONS

far the most important way of mounting guns
fighter aircraft has been to fix them to fire
ectly ahead, if necessary with their operation
chronized to the speed of the engine so that
e bullets are fired between the blades of the
opeller. Until World War II there was a belief
at guns should be aimed by a second crew
ember, usually at the upper rear, and in
itain this resulted in fighters whose sole
mament comprised four machine-guns in a
wer-driven turret. A novel British armament,
opted in 1934, was eight rifle-calibre guns
ounted in the wings; other nations used fewer
ns but relied upon 20mm cannon which in
ne cases were arranged to fire through the hub
the propeller. By 1940 Britain was switching to
nnon, deciding on four 20mm, but the United
ates preferred six or eight 0.5in and even stuck
this throughout the Korean war (1950-3). By
58, despite the technical *tour de force* of the M61
atling gun', fighters were being stripped of
ns in favour of missiles. The Vietnam war
monstrated this policy to be mistaken, and
er hanging M61 pods on external racks, the F-4
antom appeared in 1967 with an M61 under
e nose. In the F-14 Tomcat the gun is on the
t side of the nose and in the F-15 Eagle it is in
e right wing root.

OCKETS AND MISSILES

World War I scaled-up forms of firework
ckets were used against balloons and airships,
t such missiles were not used against
roplanes until the German R4/M of 55mm
libre was fired in large salvoes in 1945. Several
rman rocket tubes and recoilless guns were
ed at this time, mainly against large bombers,
d from 1950-65 the American Mighty Mouse
n-stabilized rocket of 2.75in (70mm) calibre
s a standard weapon for automatic computer-
ntrolled interceptors. Germany did not quite

get any of its World War II guided missiles into
service on fighters, but the US Air Force Falcon
series became operational in 1955, at first with
semi-active radar guidance – this homes on
reflections from the target illuminated by the
fighter's radar – and later with automatic IR
(infra-red) homing on the target's hot surfaces.
Later the short-range IR-homing Sidewinder and
much larger medium-range semi-active homing
Sparrow became available, and both now exist in
many versions. Sidewinder has four canard
control surfaces near the nose while Sparrow has
four moving wings at mid-length. The longest
ranged AAM (air-to-air missile) is the AIM-54
Phoenix with a range of over 160km (100 miles).

ELECTRONICS

Though radio communications have been
important to fighters since the end of World War
I, the science or art of electronic warfare really
dates from the first night fighters equipped with
their own radar in 1940. By 1944 the RAF was
sending large numbers of heavy bombers over
Germany each night. Their whereabouts could be
tracked by a mapping and navigation radar and a
small secondary radar, which had been specially
added as a defence against night fighters! The
Luftwaffe night fighters carried two small devices;
one automatically homed on the main RAF
radar and the other on the small defensive radar.
Only after the war did the lesson sink in that in
hostile territory any emission can be deadly.
Today missiles exist which home automatically at
high speed on any operating radar. Modern
fighters therefore attempt to minimize their own
emissions of electronic signals, while being fully
equipped with passive (listening rather than
emitting) systems that warn of illumination by
hostile radars or the launch of an enemy missile.
It is broadly possible to tell which are the serious
and effective fighters by the quality of their 'EW
suite' – their electronic-warfare installations.

In 1939 thousands of fighter pilots in most countries were fighting a rearguard action against such innovations as monoplanes, enclosed cockpits, retractable landing gear and cannon armament. Some of them flew the Fiat C.R.42 Falco (*above left*), which had none of these attributes. It only entered service with Mussolini's Regia Aeronautica in 1939, and it offered outstanding manoeuvrability and pilot view; but when it met modern monoplanes it stood little chance. This one made a raid against England in 1940 and stayed for ever, lucky to make a forced landing.

One situation where biplanes lived on was at sea, aboard aircraft carriers. In 1936 the American Grumman company began making the F4F, a new biplane fighter for the US Navy. Before the first had been completed it was redesigned as a monoplane, the F4F-2. Many orders were taken from France and Britain, and on Christmas Day 1940, an F4F-2 shot down a Ju 88 over Scotland. Until mid-1943 it was the best Allied carrier-based fighter named Wildcat (*above*). Though becoming obsolescent it was kept in production until 1945 and played a major role in the war in the Pacific.

The most important German fighter was the Messerschmitt Bf 109 (*left*). First flown in 1935, it had every advanced feature. In particular it had a small and highly loaded wing, but one which was fitted with powerful slats and flaps to give extra lift. More than 30,000 were made, no fewer than 14,112 in 1944 alone. This example was captured by the RAF.

During the early 1930s there was much earnest study to try to decide the best armament for future fighters. Some countries were turning increasingly to shell-firing cannon, while the Soviet Union conducted long experiments with large recoilless guns that could almost sink a ship. Britain eventually came up with the solution of eight ordinary machine-guns, an answer found by working out how long an enemy bomber was expected to be in the fighter's gun sights and how many bullets had to be pumped into it in that time. (Later, in 1940, Britain changed and adopted 20mm cannon.) As a sideline in 1935 the RAF issued a specification for a fighter armed with a power-driven turret with four machine-guns. The result was the Boulton Paul Defiant (*left*), which was not successful, though over one thousand were eventually built.

No fighter has ever been more famous than the British Supermarine Spitfire. None has ever been subjected to such tremendous development. The prototype, flown in March 1936, had an engine of 990hp. The first examples to reach the RAF, in 1938, had four machine-guns, but later four more were added. The aircraft had a laden weight of about 2.5 tonnes, and a speed of 560km/h (350mph). By 1942 the Mk IX (*below*) had a new Rolls-Royce Merlin engine, which gave double the power of early versions at high altitude. Despite a weight of 3.5 tonnes, the speed had jumped to 650km/h (405mph). By the war's end, when over 22,000 Spitfires and carrier-based Seafires had been built, versions were in use with over 2,000hp, weighing 5 tonnes yet able to exceed 725km/h (450mph).

In World War I many German heavy bombers and airships had raided England by night. With painful slowness methods were found of plotting the progress of the raids and eventually of intercepting them with fighters. But, especially in raids against bombers, it was a terribly chancy business that usually ended with more casualties among the night fighters – due to accidents – than to the bombers.

In 1940 the story repeated itself. The RAF just managed to fight off the mighty German Luftwaffe by day; but when the hordes of black-crossed bombers came back by night the island was all but defenceless. It was rare for an enemy bomber to be shot down. Then, again with painful slowness, the RAF learned how to use a new invention: airborne radar. Though the 'magic black boxes' were extremely temperamental, and often made crews give up in disgust, occasionally they enabled a new breed of night fighter, able to see in the dark, to shoot down enemies.

The first effective night fighter was the big and powerful Bristol Beaufighter (*top right*). An observer in a back seat studied flickering cathode-ray tubes and, if he had sufficient skill, could tell his pilot which way to steer until the pilot could make out the enemy bomber just in front. Then a burst with four cannon and six machine-guns was usually enough. By 1942 this great warplane was augmented by the de Havilland Mosquito (*bottom right*), which though made of wood was amazingly fast and versatile and soon ruled the night sky over Germany.

The only aircraft as versatile as the Mosquito was the German Junkers Ju 88 (*above*). One of its many versions was this Ju 88R-1 night fighter, whose radar aerials can be seen projecting from the nose. This one was another RAF capture. Some of the later Ju 88 night fighters were equipped with cannon mounted obliquely upward, so that by flying under a bomber's defenceless belly they could hit it by perfectly aimed no-deflection shots.

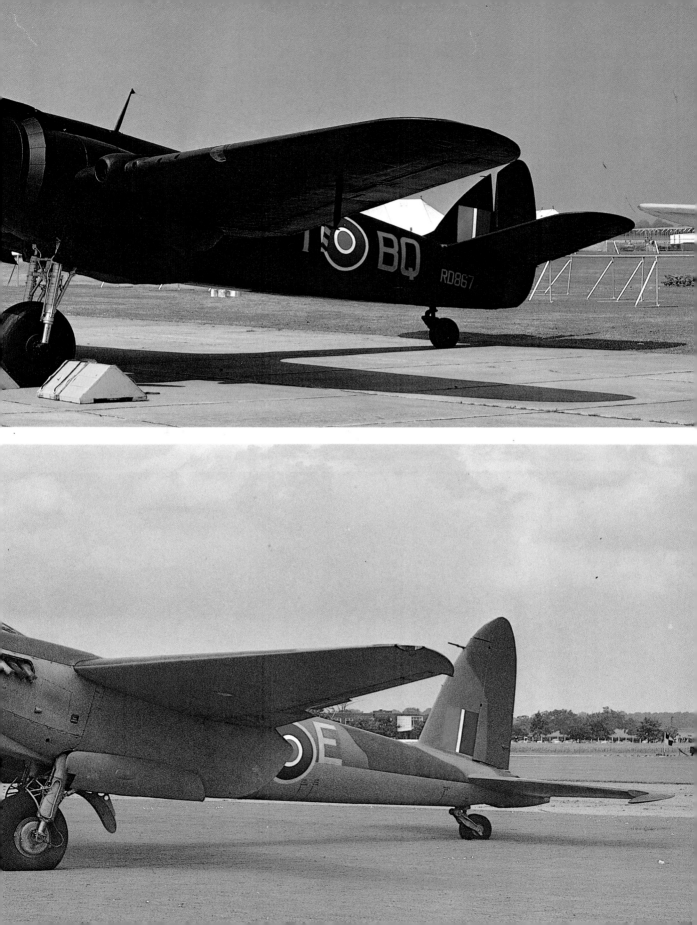

To some extent the design of a fighter is reliant upon 'trade-offs'; for example, the speed and agility of the aircraft may be gained at the expense of poor armament and a small load of fuel. For the war in the Pacific distances were reckoned on a near-global scale. By about 1942, even in the relatively small theatre of Europe, fighters were being asked to do something never before attempted – escort heavy bombers all the way to targets 1,600km (1,000miles) away and back. In the Pacific the Japanese decided one answer was fighter seaplanes, based on small islands. One example was the Kawanishi N1K1 Kyofu (mighty wind) (*above*) which reached the Imperial Navy in August 1942. For the Americans, however, there was no alternative to fighters which could carry thousands of litres of fuel. Two of the greatest were the Lockheed P-38 Lightning (*right*) and the Republic P-47 Thunderbolt (*above right*). The P-38 had two 1,000hp Allison liquid-cooled engines installed at the front of booms carrying the tail and in which were turbo superchargers and cooling radiators. Lockheed made 9,942 of these amazingly quiet fighters, but there were 15,660 Thunderbolts, popularly called Jug (from Juggernaut), powered by a Double Wasp. Both aircraft excelled in the ground-attack role.

For long-range fighting over the sea, the British Royal Navy demanded that aircraft should carry a navigator. This explains the second cockpit in the Fairey Firefly, a post-war version of which is shown overleaf. It was outclassed by single-seat land-based fighters. Today two-seat naval fighters are able to hold their own with all-comers.

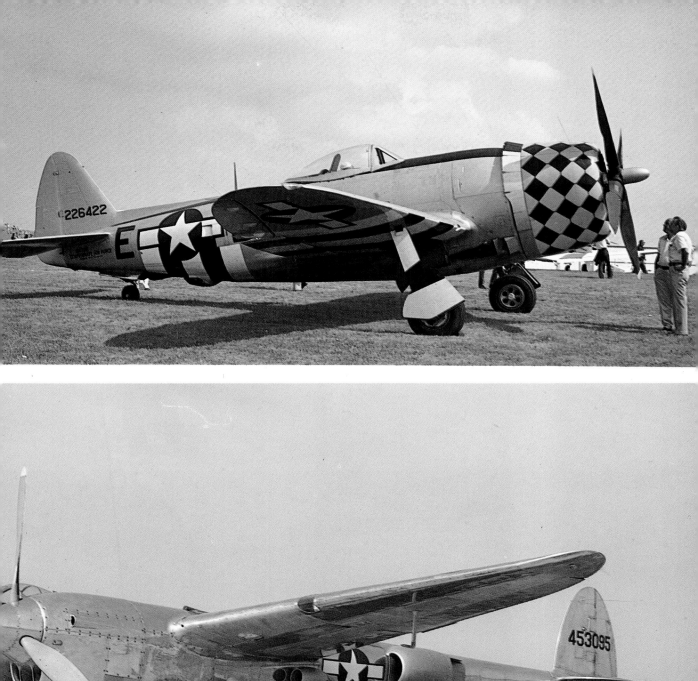

In 1945 the Allies were at last firmly on the offensive. From a position of seeming invincibility the Japanese air armadas were cut to ribbons, despite the existence of such excellent fighters as the N1K2-J Shiden-Kai (*above*). This was actually the final and simplified version of a landplane fighter derived from the Kyofu (see page 34). In terms of sheer fighting ability there was not much to choose between the N1K2-J and its American opponents, but the Japanese war machine was so shattered by late 1944 that pilots, training, fuel and even experience were in desperately short supply.

Much the same story could be told about Hitler's Germany, where not even such staggeringly formidable aircraft as the twin-jet Messerschmitt Me 262 (*above right*) could influence the course of the war. Design of the 262 and its axial jet engines began in 1938, and the prototype flew in 1941. Hitler insisted it should be a bomber, and became angry when he was told that it was a fighter; eventually it did both tasks. No fewer than 1,430 were built by May 1945, but only a few saw action.

Some 262s fell before the guns of the North American P-51 Mustang (*right*). Designed to a British requirement in 1940, the Mustang was at first ignored in its own country. Then, especially after it was re-engined with the British Merlin made in the USA by the Packard company, it was recognized as probably the best all-round fighter of the war. Goering is reported to have said: 'When I saw those P-51s over Berlin I knew the war was lost.'

After World War II Britain devoted little attention to defence equipment and lagged behind other countries, except in jet engines where for a time British makes were supreme. No modern fighters were put into service in the decade following the war, the wartime Vampire and Meteor having to soldier on into the mid-1950s. Though a Gloster design, the Meteor was developed into a primitive night fighter by the sister firm of Armstrong Whitworth, the ultimate model being the NF.14 (*below*). Its technology was identical with that of wartime night fighters. The aircraft shown is brightly painted as a navigation trainer.

In contrast, the US Air Force, formed in 1947, thrust forward in every way possible. For all-weather interception it contracted with Hughes Aircraft for a computerized system linking radar with the flight controls so that the pilot did not need to see the target at all. A salvo of rockets was fired automatically to the place in the sky where the target would be at the time. The system was even fitted into the small F-86 Sabre, resulting in the F-86D (*right*), a transonic single-seater of which 2,504 were built. NATO nations received a simpler version with guns instead of rockets. The F-86D gained world speed records at 1,123 and 1,151km/h (698 and 715mph).

The first supersonic fighter in Western Europe was France's Dassault Super Mystère B2 (top left), the last of a series of progressively more advanced fighters of conventional design which began with the Ouragan (Hurricane) of 1949. Though it could reach Mach 1.125 on the level, the 'SMB2' as it was popularly called was phased out in 1959 in favour of the radical Mirage IIIC, and only 180 were built. Totally different in size, power and technology is the outstanding McDonnell Douglas F-15 Eagle (*above*). The Eagle was designed to beat the incredibly fast but specialized MiG-25 'Foxbat' and is a splendid all-round performer with exceptional flight performance and a modern combination of electronics and weapons. But in many respects it is surpassed by the latest of all interceptors, the Panavia Tornado F.2 (*left*), 165 of which are being built for the RAF. Though it is as fast as an Eagle, this swing-wing fighter (see page 61) has much smaller engines and thus has greater range and endurance for any given amount of fuel. It carries an additional crew member to manage the extremely advanced electronics. The four missiles carried in this picture are the British Sky Flash, the most formidable medium-range weapon available.

FIGHTER/BOMBERS

One of the first services to make fighters carry bombs was the US Navy, and most naval jet fighters have been able to fly attack missions. An especially graceful type of the immediate post-war era was this Royal Navy Sea Hawk, a Hawker design developed and manufactured by Armstrong Whitworth.

INDEX

References in italics are to illustrations

Acknowledgements

Unless otherwise mentioned all photographs provided by Mike Hooks.

Air Portraits Colour Library contents, 24-25; Mike Jerram 4-5, 13 above; MAP 39 above, 60, 62-63 below; Photri title page; Tabby (R A Nicholls/Aviation Photographs International) 7 above, (R A Nicholls) 58-59 above, (R A Nicholls/Aviation Photographs International/J K Flack) 60-61 below; Michael Taylor 8-9, (Gordon Bain) 10 above, (Gordon S Williams) 10-11 below, (Gordon S Williams) 19 above, 20 below, 21 below, 26 above, 28-29 below, 30 above left, 32 above, 34 above, 35 above – 38 above, 40-41, 44-45 below, 52 above, 52-53 below, 54 above, 56-57, 58-59 below, 61 above, 63 above.

FRONT COVER PHOTOGRAPH:
TRH PICTURES/USAF
BACK COVER PHOTOGRAPH:
QUADRANT PICTURE LIBRARY/
FLIGHT

This edition published in 1990 by Treasure Press, Michelin House, 81 Fulham Road, London SW3 6RB

© 1981 Octopus Books Limited

ISBN 1 85051 483 6

Produced by Mandarin Offset
Printed in Hong Kong